Light and Sound

KINGFISHER

Kingfisher Publications Plc
New Penderel House
283–288 High Holborn
London WC1V 7HZ
www.kingfisherpub.com

First published by Kingfisher Publications Plc 2007
2 4 6 8 10 9 7 5 3 1
1TR/1106/PROSP/RNB/140MA/F

A CIP catalogue record for this book is available from the British Library.

ISBN 978 0 7534 1377 7

Senior editor: Belinda Weber
Designer: Rebecca Johns
Cover designer: Poppy Jenkins
Picture research manager: Cee Weston-Baker
DTP co-ordinator: Catherine Hibbert
Production controller: Jessamy Oldfield
Indexer: Hilary Bird

Printed in China

Acknowledgements
The publishers would like to thank the following for permission to reproduce their material. Every care has been taken
to trace copyright holders. However, if there have been unintentional omissions or failure to trace copyright holders,
we apologise and will, if informed, endeavour to make corrections in any future edition.
b = bottom, c = centre, l = left, t = top, r = right

Pages: cover Alamy/Stockbyte; 1 Alamy/Stockbyte; 2–3 Corbis; 4–5 Corbis/Zefa; 6–7 Getty/Stone; 7 Science Photo Library (SPL)/
Larry Landolfi; 8l Corbis/Randy Farris; 9tr Getty/Stone; 9bl Natural History Picture Agency/James Carmichael Jr; 10–11 Alamy/Stock
Connection; 12c Corbis/Walter Hodges; 12–13 Corbis/Zefa; 13t Nature Picture Library/David Shale; 14 Corbis; 15t Getty/Stone;
15b SPL; 16 Corbis/Aaron Horowitz; 17t SPL/Celestial Image Co.; 17b Nature Picture Library/Jorma Luhta; 18–19 Corbis;
19tl Alamy/Phototake Inc.; 20 Corbis/RoyMorsch; 21t Alamy/Imageshopstop; 21b SPL/Lawrence Lawry; 22 Getty/Photographer's Choice;
23t Alamy/Sami Sarkis; 23b SPL/NASA; 24 Brand X Pictures; 25t Corbis/NASA; 25b SPL/Custom Medical Stock Photo; 26 Alamy/Oote Boe;
27t SPL/Merlin Tuttle; 27 SPL; 28 Alamy/A T Willett; 28t Alamy/Imagestate; 30–31 Alamy/Butch Martin; 31c Corbis/Zefa; 32br
Getty/Imagebank; 32–33 Corbis/Zefa; 33t Getty/Imagebank; 34 Corbis/Bill Ross; 35bl Getty/Imagebank; 35r Corbis/Carmen Redondo;
36 Frank Lane Picture Agency/David Hosking; 37 Corbis; 37br Getty/Photodisc Red; 38 Getty/Johner Images; 39tl Alamy/Profimedia; 39b
Getty/Photonica; 40l Photolibrary.com; 40r Corbis; 41t SPL/Hank Morgan; 41b SPL/NASA; 48 Corbis/Pat Doyle

Illustrations on pages: 8, 30 Sebastien Quigley (Linden Artists); 10, 11 Encompass Graphics

Commissioned photography on pages 42–47 by Andy Crawford
Project-maker and photoshoot co-ordinator: Jane Thomas
Thank you to models Mary Conquest, Darius Caple,
Jamie Chang-Leng and Georgina Page

KFYK Kingfisher Young Knowledge

Light and Sound

Dr Mike Goldsmith

Contents

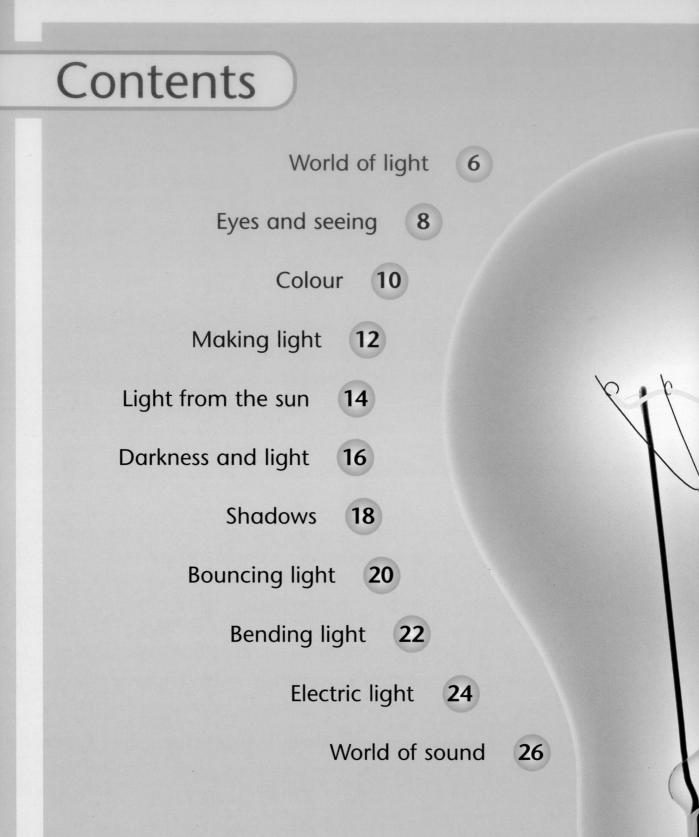

World of light 6

Eyes and seeing 8

Colour 10

Making light 12

Light from the sun 14

Darkness and light 16

Shadows 18

Bouncing light 20

Bending light 22

Electric light 24

World of sound 26

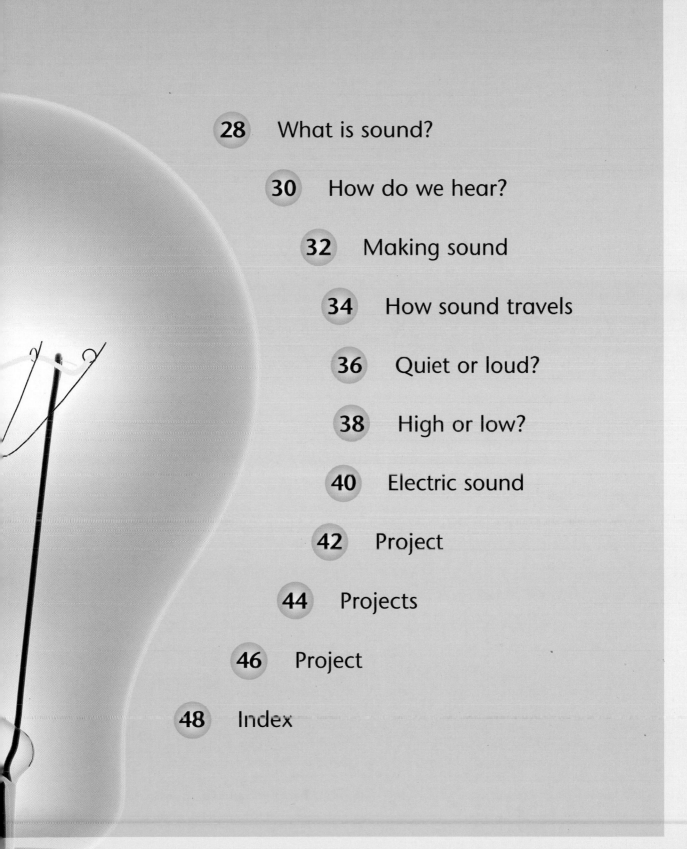

28 What is sound?

30 How do we hear?

32 Making sound

34 How sound travels

36 Quiet or loud?

38 High or low?

40 Electric sound

42 Project

44 Projects

46 Project

48 Index

6) World of **light**

We need light to live. It gives us day and night, colours, pictures, stars and rainbows. We also use it to play CDs and make electricity.

The bright sun

The sun is a star. It is a huge ball of burning gas that gives us light and warmth. Without it, there would not be any life on earth.

gas – *a shapeless substance, such as air, that is not solid or liquid*

Looking at the stars

Using telescopes, scientists can see more light from the stars. They can work out how far away from earth they are, how hot they are and what they are made of.

telescope – *an invention that makes things look bigger*

Eyes and seeing

People need light to be able to see. Many night-time animals can see with less light than we need. They have big eyes, which take in as much light as possible.

retina

iris

pupil

lens

How people see

Light bounces off objects and into the eye through the pupil. The lens focuses the light on the retina and the brain works out what you are seeing.

iris – *the coloured part of the eye*

Animal eyes

Night-time animals, like this owl, have huge eyes. They can see well in the dark and hunt at night.

eyes

Spider eyes

Spiders are hunters and need to catch insects to eat. Many spiders have eight eyes, and they can see in all directions at once.

retina – a special layer at the back of the eye that picks up light

Colour

People can see millions of different colours. Colours mix in different ways – all pigments mixed together make black, and all colours of lights mixed together make white.

blue paint

yellow and blue mix to make green

red, yellow and blue mix to make black

red and blue mix to make purple

yellow paint

red and yellow mix to make orange

red paint

Mixing pigments

The colours of paints and dyes are made by mixing pigments. All colours other than red, yellow and blue can be made by mixing.

pigments – substances that give something its colour

green light

red light

all colours of light
mixed together
make white

green and
red mix to
make yellow

red and blue mix
to make magenta

blue and
green mix to
make cyan

blue light

Mixing lights
Lights mix in a different
way to pigments.
All colours are made
by mixing different
amounts of red, blue
and green light.

Separating light
Sunlight (white light) is a
mixture of colours. Raindrops
separate these colours to
make a rainbow of red,
orange, yellow, green,
blue, indigo and violet.

separating – splitting apart

Making light

Anything will shine with light if it gets hot enough. Most of the light we see comes from hot objects, such as the sun, light bulbs and stars.

Electric light

Some substances glow with light when electricity passes through them. When electricity is passed through neon gas, it gives coloured light that can be used in advertising signs.

neon – *an invisible gas that glows when electricity passes through it*

Living light

Some deep-sea fish make light from chemicals in their bodies. They use their light to catch food.

Birthday lights

Flames give off light as well as heat. The candles on this birthday cake glow brightly as they burn.

chemicals – substances that combine and react with each other

Light from the sun

For billions of years, the sun's light has shone on our world. It is millions of kilometres away, yet it is dangerous to look at it directly.

Life from light

Every living thing on earth needs sunlight. The leaves of plants trap sunlight to grow.

liquid – a runny substance

Glowing sunsets

As the earth turns, the sun moves across the sky. When the sun is low in the sky, it looks red because its light passes through the thick, dusty air near the ground.

Keeping warm

Heat from the sun keeps the earth's oceans liquid. Without it, all the water and air around the planet would be frozen.

land

ocean

frozen – *turned to ice*

Darkness and light

When there is no light, we see darkness. Our planet spins in space – when it turns away from the sun, it is night. We need other sources of light to see in the dark.

Moonlight

The moon does not make its own light. Sunlight bounces off it and makes it glow.

source – where something comes from; for example, the sun is a source of light

Stars

Stars make their own light. Many are brighter than our star, the sun. They look very faint because they are so far away.

Nature's light show

The sun sends out particles that carry electricity. These can bounce off particles in the air, making the sky glow with different colours.

particles – extremely small pieces

Shadows

When something blocks light, it casts a shadow. It is cooler and darker in the shadows because they are cut off from the sun's warmth and light.

Shadows

All solid objects cast shadows. They may be long or short, depending on how the sunlight falls on them.

blocks – *gets in the way of*

Darkness by day

Sometimes the moon passes between the earth and the sun. It blocks our view of the sun, causing darkness. This is called a solar eclipse.

solar – *to do with the sun*

Bouncing light

Light bounces off most objects. A lot of light bounces off snow, so it shines bright in sunlight. Coal hardly lets any light bounce back from it, so it is dark.

Seeing double

The surface of a mirror is so smooth that it bounces back light in exactly the same pattern as it receives it. This is called a reflection.

reflection – *the image of what is in front of a mirror*

Bright nights

In this picture, the sun's light has bounced off the moon to the sea, making the sea shine with light.

Talking with light

Light can travel through glass threads called optical fibres. These fibres can carry telephone calls and computer signals.

optical fibres – thin threads of glass along which light can pass

Bending light

Objects that light can travel through are called transparent. When light enters a transparent substance – such as glass or water – it bends.

Funny shapes

When light travels between water and air it bends, and what we see seems out of shape. The bending light has made this boy's body look bigger in the water.

transparent – see-through, or clear

Transparent life

Some sea creatures, like this jellyfish, are transparent. It makes them very hard to see in the deep and murky waters.

Bigger and brighter

Magnifying lenses are fatter in the middle. They bend the light and make things look bigger than they are.

magnifying – *making something seem bigger than it is*

Electric light

Light can make electricity and electricity can make light. In a light bulb, electricity heats up a thin wire so that it glows.

Electric light

By colouring the glass of these light bulbs, different coloured lights are produced. Light bulbs get hot when switched on, so do not touch them.

produced – *made*

Solar power

Solar panels outside this space station collect sunlight and turn it into electricity. The electricity is then used as power.

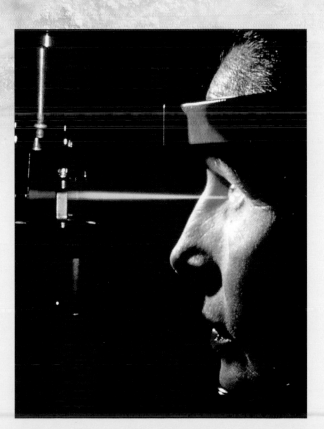

Laser surgery

Very narrow beams of light, called lasers, can be used for many things. They can be for delicate operations, such as eye surgery.

delicate – *needing or using great care*

World of sound

There are sounds all around us. We listen to music and hear voices. Sound has many other uses, too. It can 'draw' pictures and help animals to find their prey.

Unwelcome sounds
Sounds that are unpleasant to listen to, such as the sound of heavy drills, are called noise.

unwelcome – not wanted

Sounds in the dark

Bats use sound to hunt.
They give a shrill call
that bounces off any
solid object. They hear
the echo and work out
where their food is.

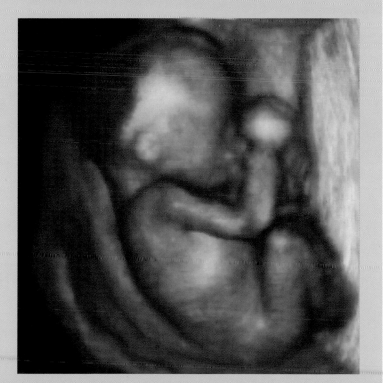

Sounds healthy

Doctors use sound
to create pictures of
unborn babies. Sound
waves bounce off the
baby, and computers
can 'draw' the picture.

echo – a sound that bounces off an object

What is sound?

Sound is a sort of wave or ripple. Like ripples in a pond, sound travels in all directions. The sounds get quieter the further you are from their source.

Boom!

Some planes travel faster than sound. They make a shock wave in the air. This can be heard as a loud bang, called a sonic boom.

sonic boom – *the noise created when something travels faster than sound*

Silent space

Sound can travel through air or water. There is no air or water in space so there is no sound.

Sound speeds

Sound travels quicker through water than through air. These orca use clicks and whistles to communicate underwater.

communicate – *to send a message to another creature*

How do we hear?

When sound enters the ear, it travels down a tube. The tube's end is covered by a very thin wall of skin, called the eardrum.

tiny bones

ear tube or canal

nerve

eardrum

Inside the ear

When a sound hits the eardrum, it wobbles and makes the tiny bones inside the ear vibrate.

vibrate – *to move rapidly to and fro*

Hearing

Nerves in the ear send messages to the brain. The brain works out what sound is being heard.

Animal ears

Most animals can hear, but few have ears like ours. The fennec fox has huge ears. They can turn round to pick up the slightest sound.

nerves – special fibres that run from the brain to all parts of the body

Making sound

Sound is usually made when something moves backwards and forwards very quickly. The moving thing might be a leaf in the breeze, the metal of a bell or a guitar string.

Musical sounds

Blowing a trumpet makes a buzzing sound in the mouthpiece. This sound travels through the trumpet to make music.

mouthpiece – the part that goes over, or into, the mouth

Voices

When you speak or sing, two flaps of skin in your throat wobble. These are called vocal cords.

Snaps and crackles

Sound can be a burst, like a balloon popping or fireworks exploding. We hear the crackles and fizzes while watching the lights.

vocal cords – flaps of skin that enable humans to speak

How sound travels

Sounds travel as waves through air, water or solid objects. The waves eventually die away, but they can cover great distances first.

Long journeys

A busy street is a noisy place. The sounds of people talking, and cars and other vehicles can travel a long way.

vehicles – anything used for transporting people or things

Echoes

Sound waves bounce
back from hard objects,
like walls. We call
these sounds echoes.

*the echo bounces
off the cave wall
and the same shout
is heard again*

child shouts

Quiet or loud?

The more a sound wave wobbles, the louder it sounds. One of the loudest natural sounds is when a volcano erupts. Bombs and rocket engines make the loudest human sounds.

Shhh...

Some animals can hear sounds that are too quiet for people. An aardvark can hear termites crawling under the ground.

natural – *occurring in nature, not made by people or machines*

Ouch!

Very loud sounds can damage your ears. Our ears tense up when they hear loud noises, making everything sound muffled.

damage – to hurt or cause injury

High or low?

Sound waves wobble at different speeds. The faster the sound waves wobble, the higher the sound they produce. Sounds that wobble slower are lower.

Making music

Violin strings move quickly and make a high sound. Most guitar strings move more slowly so their sound is lower.

produce – to make, or create

High mews and low roars

Kittens have small vocal cords and weak lungs so they make high, quiet mews. Lions are big cats with powerful lungs. They make low, loud roars.

lungs – *the parts inside the body that are used for breathing*

Sound can be changed into electricity. The electricity can then be changed back into sounds again. This happens when you speak on the telephone.

Microphones

A microphone changes sound into a wobbling pattern of electricity. A loudspeaker turns these patterns back into sounds.

loudspeaker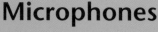

microphone

__loudspeaker__ – a device that changes electricity into sound

Changing sound

By turning sounds into pictures like this one, scientists can see what we hear. These pictures are called sonograms.

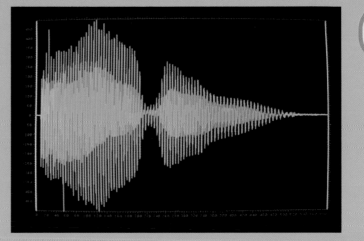

Voices from space

When astronauts are outside the spacecraft, they communicate using microphones and loudspeakers.

sonogram – *a computer-generated picture of a sound*

Shadow puppets

Make animal puppets

Solid shapes block the light and cast shadows. You can make different shaped shadows, like this dragon, and put on a shadow puppet show.

You will need

- Pencil
- Coloured paper
- Scissors
- Sweet wrappers
- Sticky tape
- Drinking straw or stick
- Torch

1 Draw a dragon with a long pointed tail, feet and an open mouth on coloured paper.

2 Carefully cut out the dragon with scissors. Ask an adult to help with the tricky bits.

3 On one side, stick sweet wrappers to makes flames coming out of the dragon's mouth.

You can make other shadow puppets, like a cat or a bird.

4 Tape a drinking straw or short stick to the back. Turn the dragon over and draw an eye, nose and wings.

5 In a darkened room, ask a friend to shine a torch on to a plain wall. This will make shadows.

Position your shadow puppet in front of the torch and move it around in the light.

Shadow clock

Tell the time by shadows

Shadow clocks measure time
using shadows cast by the sun.
Have fun making your own clock.

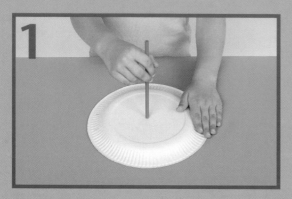

1

Make a small hole in the middle
of a paper plate and stand a
drinking straw upright in the hole.

You will need
- Paper plate
- Drinking straw
- Felt-tip pens

*Keep your clock in the same place,
and when the shadows fall, you'll
be able to tell the time.*

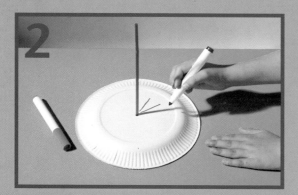

2

Put the plate in a sunlit place.
Every hour, draw a line along
the shadow the straw makes
and note the time.

Xylophone

Make music
You can make a simple xylophone with glasses of water and a wooden spoon.

You will need
- 5 glasses, all the same
- Jug of water
- Food colouring
- Wooden spoon

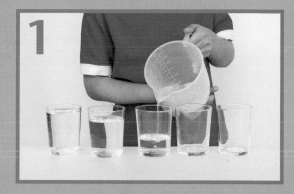

Line the glasses up and pour water into them. Fill the first right to the top, then the rest with a little less than the one before.

You can add a few drops of different food colourings to the glasses to colour the water.

Gently tap each glass with the spoon and you will hear that each one makes a different sound.

Plastic cup telephone

Make a working phone

You can make sound travel along a piece of stretched-out string. The plastic cups work as the microphone and the loudspeaker so that you can hear what your friend is saying.

You will need
- 2 plastic cups
- Stickers and coloured paper
- Scissors
- Modelling clay
- Sharp pencil
- Piece of string, 4–6 metres long

1

Decorate two clean, empty plastic cups with stickers and shapes cut from different coloured paper.

The sound of your voice travels along the string.

2

Place a ball of modelling clay under each cup and make a hole in the bottom with a sharp pencil.

3

Thread one end of the string through the hole, then tie a knot at the end.

4

Do the same with the other cup. Give a friend one cup and stretch out the string. Talk into the cup.

If your friend holds the other cup to his ear, he will hear what you are saying.

Index

animals 9, 27, 31, 36, 39

bending light 22–23

brain 8, 31

candles 13

colours 10–11

darkness 16–17

ears 30–31

echoes 35

electricity 12, 24–25,
    40–41

eyes 8–9

fish 13

hearing 30–31

lasers 25

loudspeakers 40, 41

magnifying lenses 23

microphones 40, 41

mirrors 20

moon 16, 19, 21

music 26, 32, 38, 45

night 16

noise 26

optical fibres 21

puppets 42–43

rainbows 11

reflections 20

shadows 18–19, 42–43, 44

solar power 25

sonic boom 28

sonograms 41

sound waves 27, 28, 34–35,
    36, 38

stars 6, 7, 12, 17

sun 6, 11, 12, 14–15, 18–19,
    21, 44

telephones 40, 46–47

telescopes 7

television 11

transparent objects 22–23

voices 26, 33

water 22–23, 29, 45

xylophone 45